Twenty Little Triangle Quilts

With Full-Size Templates

Gwen Marston

Instructions and Illustrations by Pat Holly

DOVER PUBLICATIONS, INC.
Mineola, New York

Acknowledgments

The Linden Mill quilt was made by Mary Schafer.
All other quilts were designed and made by Gwen Marston.
All illustrations and instructions by Pat Holly.
Photographs by The Keva Partnership.

Dedication

This book is dedicated to Brenda and Matthew

Other Books by the Author

* = co-authored by Joe Cunningham.
American Beauties: Rose and Tulip Quilts. American Quilter's Society, Paducah, Kentucky, 1988.
Amish Quilting Patterns. Dover Publications, Inc., New York, 1987.
Liberated Quiltmaking. American Quilter's Society, 1996.
Mary Schafer and Her Quilts. Michigan State University Press, East Lansing, Michigan, 1987.
Q is For Quilt. Michigan State University Press, 1987.
Quilting With Style: Principles for Great Pattern Design. American Quilter's Society, 1993.
Sets and Borders. American Quilter's Society, 1987.
70 Classic Quilting Patterns. Dover Publications, Inc., 1987.
Twenty Little Amish Quilts. Dover Publications, Inc., 1993.
Twenty Little Four-Patch Quilts. Dover Publications, Inc., 1996.
Twenty Little Log Cabin Quilts. Dover Publications, Inc., 1995.
Twenty Little Patchwork Quilts. Dover Publications, Inc., 1990.
Twenty Little Pinwheel Quilts. Dover Publications, Inc., 1994.

Bibliographical Note

Twenty Little Triangle Quilts: With Full-Size Templates is a new work, first published by Dover Publications, Inc., in 1997.

Library of Congress Cataloging-in-Publication Data

Marston, Gwen.
    Twenty little triangle quilts / Gwen Maston; instructions and illustrations by Pat Holly.
      p.   cm.
    ISBN 0-486-29700-4 (pbk.)
     1. Patchwork—Patterns.   2. Patchwork quilts.   3. Miniature quilts.   I. Title.
TT835.M2729 1997
46.46'041—dc21   97-7959
                                                          CIP

Manufactured in the United States of America
Dover Publications, Inc., 31 East 2nd Street, Mineola, N.Y. 11501

Introduction

You might think that restricting yourself to making quilts with just triangles would be limiting. It isn't. Triangles come in many shapes *(Figure 1)*, and there are a surprising number of ways to arrange triangles to create both block and all-over patterns. Because of this flexibility, working with triangles can produce many different effects. Making this batch of Twenty Little Triangle quilts was really enjoyable and entertaining. Once I got started, I had a hard time keeping up with the ideas that presented themselves to me as I worked.

With the exception of Linden Mill, which was made by Mary Schafer, I made all of these triangle quilts. They are a part of my collection of over 250 small quilts. Working on a small scale has made it possible for me to experiment with many different designs and artistic ideas. While I still enjoy making full-size quilts, these little ones seem to keep popping out too.

Figure 1

Triangles - separated by comparing sides

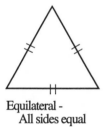 

Equilateral -
All sides equal

Isosceles -
Two sides equal

Scalene -
No sides equal

Triangles - separated by comparing angles

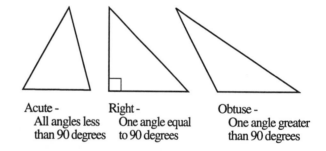

Acute -
All angles less
than 90 degrees

Right -
One angle equal
to 90 degrees

Obtuse -
One angle greater
than 90 degrees

General Instructions

Fabric

One aspect of working on a small scale is that you can explore a wide variety of fabrics. This is especially true when you are making scrap quilts.

I used 100% cotton in all of these triangle quilts. Because of the small size, not much fabric is required. Most of us who make quilts have an ample supply of scraps left over from other projects. If you want to buy new fabric, a selection of fat quarters is perfect for small quilts. This is an economical way to expand your fabric collection and most quilt shops have a spectacular collection of fat quarters. The only larger piece that is required is for the backing, and three quarters of a yard is adequate for any of these quilts.

I always wash fabric before using it. While most fabrics today are colorfast, not all are. A second reason I wash fabric before I use it in a quilt is because washing removes the sizing and makes hand-quilting easier. Once

the fabrics have been washed, iron them so they will lie flat when you cut out the patches. Thorough pressing is the first step towards accurate cutting.

Templates

When quilters use the word template, they are referring to the patterns used to make quilts. Accurate templates are the prerequisite to accurate piecing. The templates required to make all of these quilts are printed on lightweight cardboard in the center of this book. They are full-size and can be used for either hand- or machine-piecing. For hand-piecing, you can use them just as they are. For machine-piecing, add ¼" seam allowance around each template. Notice that the templates each have an arrow on them, indicating which side of the triangle should be placed on the straight grain of the fabric. Keeping all of the outside edges of the block on the straight grain will help keep your quilt square.

Cutting the Patches

There are a number of systems for making half-square triangles. If you use the template method, draw around the template on the wrong side of your fabric with a sharp pencil. To make the construction faster, you can layer the fabric and cut four patches at a time very accurately. It is important to make sure that the fabric is well pressed and that all four layers are lying flat. Newer methods for cutting triangles include the bias-strip method, and drawing grid lines on the back of the fabric, sewing and cutting. These two methods are not detailed in this book, but are available in other books.

My favorite method is to work with individual patches and to cut the patches with a rotary cutter. I layer the fabric, cut strips, then cut squares and finally cut the squares diagonally to produce the patches. I like this system best because it gives me total flexibility in choosing color combinations as I work, because I think it is faster than the other systems and because I can do it with a high degree of accuracy as well.

Rotary cutting triangles is quick, easy and accurate. You can layer the fabric and cut four layers at a time if you like. Remember to press the fabric and make sure it is lying flat. There are two different formulas for cutting right triangles: one for triangles that have the short side on the straight grain and another for triangles that have the long side on the straight grain. The templates give you the finished size of each patch, so you can check your rotary-cut triangles against them.

If the short sides of the triangle are to be on the straight grain, add ⅞" to the finished size of the triangle, cut squares that size and then cut the squares in half diagonally *(Figure 2)*.

If the long side of the triangle is to be on the straight grain, add 1¼" to the finished size of the triangle, cut squares that size and quarter them diagonally *(Figure 3)*.

As you cut, check every so often to make sure the fabric is still squared up. When you first square up the fabric, fold the selvage sides together. I often fold the fabric one more time, so that it is in fourths, since it is easier to hold the ruler steady for a short cut than for a long cut.

Figure 3

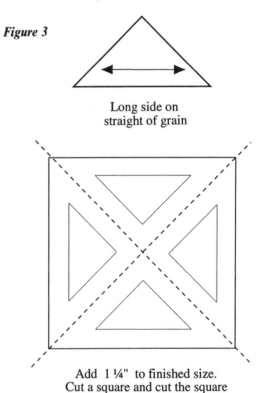

Long side on
straight of grain

Add 1¼" to finished size.
Cut a square and cut the square
in fourths diagonally.

Figure 2

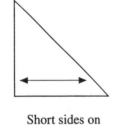

Short sides on
straight of grain

Add 7/8" to finished size.
Cut a square this size.
Cut the square diagonally in half.

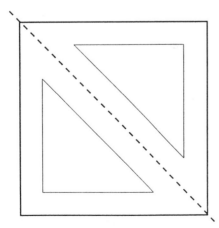

Place the fabric with the end you are planning to square up on the right, then line up the crosswise grid of your ruler with the folded edge of the fabric (the selvage side is not always straight and is therefore less reliable). Once you have squared the ends of the fabric, turn it around so that the squared edge is on your left. Turn the fabric carefully so the edges stay aligned.

Here are a few tips to successful rotary cutting:

1. Always be safe. The rotary cutter is very sharp, so use it carefully.

2. Get in the habit of closing the blade *every* time you lay the cutter down.
3. Keep a sharp blade in the cutter.
4. If you are right-handed, place the fabric on the cutting mat so it extends to the right.
5. Use a ruler and a cutting mat that both have vertical and horizontal grids marked on them. These lines will help you cut strips that are straight and accurate.
6. Always cut away from yourself, never toward yourself.
7. Hold the ruler firmly with your left hand.
8. Square up the uneven raw edges.
9. Position the ruler to the proper width and cut the fabric with one clean stroke.

Standard Block Construction

Once you have the patches cut out, you are ready to begin sewing the blocks together. Set the stitch length on your sewing machine at 10 to 12 stitches per inch. When you sew, make sure you are sewing a consistent ¼" seam. The plate on most sewing machines is marked with a ¼" seam allowance. To increase accuracy, place several layers of masking tape or moleskin (an adhesive product sold to comfort tender spots on feet) on the sewing machine plate exactly ¼" away from the needle.

With right sides together, sew the triangles into rows, then sew the rows together into blocks.

Working with Triangles

Triangles are tricky, because at least one side, and sometimes two sides, are on the bias. Learning how to work with triangles is important if the quilts you make are to work out for you. Here are some triangle tips to make your work go smoothly and successfully:

1. When sewing two bias edges together, line up the patches and feed them carefully through the machine so you don't stretch them.
2. Decide on how you are going to sew the triangles together and do it the same way throughout the process. Being consistent will protect you from turning a unit the wrong way. For example, if you decide to place the dark triangle on the bottom, do so all the time.
3. Watch the end of the triangle as it goes through the machine. This is where the trouble can occur, as the triangle can veer off slightly at the end, resulting in an inaccurate seam allowance.
4. Small triangles can be hard to handle. They are hard to pick up, line up and feed evenly through the machine. For half-square triangles, I found that if I cut strips, put a light and dark strip right sides together, press them and then cut them, they are already lined up. If you handle them gently, they will stay lined up as you chain piece them together.

Chain Piecing

Whether or not you use standard block construction, you can chain piece the units together. Join two units and, without cutting the thread, feed two more through the sewing machine. You can sew many units together, one right after the other, without cutting the thread between them (see *Figure 4*). This makes construction move along faster and also saves thread. Once you have sewn many units together, remove them from the sewing machine and cut them apart.

Figure 4

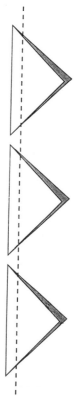

Adding the Borders

Dimensions for cutting the borders are provided in the instructions for every quilt. Each of us sews a little bit differently, however, so it's a good idea to wait until your quilt is pieced before cutting the borders. The most accurate way to measure for borders is to measure through the middle of your quilt as shown in *Figure 5*. A good rule that I learned from carpenters is to "measure twice and cut once."

Add the borders to the long sides of your quilt first. Pin both ends and then the midpoint of the border. Place additional pins about every 2" between these first pins. Careful measuring and pinning is the way to make sure your borders lie flat and don't waffle. It is worth taking the extra time and care to make sure you get the borders sewn on right the first time.

Once all four borders are sewn on, take the time to press the entire quilt top carefully. This will make the job of marking the quilting designs on the quilt much easier.

Figure 5

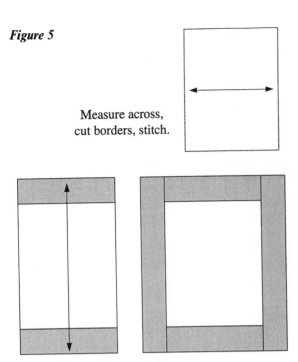

Measure across,
cut borders, stitch.

Measure length, cut borders, stitch.

Quilting Designs

The quilting designs on these small triangle quilts are very simple. There isn't much room on small quilts to do a lot of quilting, nor is it necessary to quilt fancy designs on them. The most logical way to quilt triangles is to outline each one. If the triangles are extra small, quilting just the long side of each triangle makes sense. Sashing's can be "X-ed," and simple diagonals work nicely on the borders.

You do not even need to mark the quilting lines on the triangles. They are small and you can "eyeball" them easily. For marking other parts of the quilt, I like to use a silver Berol Verithin pencil because it shows up on all fabrics, makes a fine line, is safe for all fabrics and washes out. You can buy Berol Verithin pencils in most quilt shops. If you can't find one there, check your local art supply or office supply store.

Backing

You can use a fabric from your quilt top for the backing, or use something entirely different. You might even decide to piece the backing from several interesting fabrics. This is an old idea that has again become popular with today's quilters.

Cut the backing about 1½" larger than the quilt top on all four sides.

Batting

My preference is to use a thin cotton batting in small quilts. While cotton is a little harder to hand-quilt, I like

the flat look and the feel you get with cotton. There are a number of different brands on the market. Try several different ones to determine which you like the best. If you prefer polyester batting, make sure you select one that is thin. Some polyester batts seem too puffy, especially when used in small quilts.

Lay your quilt top on the batting, and cut the batting just slightly larger than the top.

The Quilting Frame

Most quilters today quilt in a hoop. You will need to baste all three layers together before putting your quilt in a hoop. If you quilt in a hoop, it is recommended that you begin quilting in the middle and work outward.

For both quilting and basting, I get the best results from stretching the quilt in a full-size frame that I make myself. It is simply four 1" x 2" pine boards about 36" long. Staple a length of sturdy fabric to all four boards. Position the fabric so it extends about ½" over the long edge of the boards.

Baste the edges of the quilt backing to two of the boards, lay these across the other two boards and secure them with small C-clamps. Pin the two loose edges of the quilt backing to the fabric strips every 1" to 2". Spread the batting over the backing and smooth it out. Lay the quilt top on the batting and pin around all four edges through all the layers. Check to make sure the quilt is stretched tightly and that there are no wrinkles in the backing or the top.

In this kind of frame, you start quilting around the edges and work toward the center of the quilt. You do not have to worry about working in fullness as you do when using a hoop. If you can't reach the center, remove the clamps, roll the quilt up on the boards and re-clamp.

Quilting in a full-size frame results in quilts that lie perfectly flat because even tension is maintained throughout the entire quilting process.

Hand Quilting

The quilting stitch is a small running stitch that holds all three layers of the quilt together. It is done with a single strand of cotton quilting thread and a short needle called a "between." The larger the number of the needle, the smaller the needle. I use a number 9 between for all of my quilting. Experiment with different sizes until you find one that feels right for you. There are a variety of quilting needles available today. Look for ones that have eyes that are easy to thread. There is quite a variation from one brand to another. There are also a number of different quilting threads available today. I prefer one that is treated with a glazed coating that makes it easy to thread on the needle and helps prevent unwanted knotting.

The needle is guided through the layers of the quilt by a thimble on the middle finger of the right hand. The left hand is underneath the quilt so that it can feel the needle as it goes through all three layers. The quilting stitch is done in a rocking motion, up and down, building 4 to 6 stitches on the needle before it is pulled through. Describing this technique is difficult. The best way to learn to quilt is to find someone who can sit with you and show you how. Learning to do it correctly to begin with will save you a lot of grief. Quilting is like learning to ride a bicycle—once you learn you never forget.

When I first learned to quilt my Mennonite teachers told me to try to get the stitches even and not to worry if they weren't as small as I wanted them to be. "That will come in time," they told me. This is good advice.

Binding

Once your quilt is quilted, you are ready to finish the edges. There are many ways to finish the edges of a quilt. I will explain how I make a single, separate continuous binding cut on the straight of the fabric. This is my favorite way to bind a quilt. I think a single binding is preferable to a double binding, particularly on small quilts, because it is finer and the scale is more suitable to small quilts.

Begin by folding the fabric in four layers. Square up the end of the fabric and cut two 1¼"-wide strips with your rotary cutter. Two strips of 45"-wide fabric will make enough binding for any of these small quilts.

Sew the two strips together and finger-press the seams open. This will make the join less visible, as the extra fabric in the seam allowance is divided equally on both sides. Begin stitching the binding to the quilt in the middle of the side. Never start in the corner as this makes turning the corners almost impossible. Lay the binding along the edge of the quilt top with the right sides together. Start sewing on the binding, leaving about 3" of the binding loose. This is so you can make a final joining seam that lays flat and is identical to all other joining seams. This method gives much nicer results than the system where the ends are overlapped, creating extra fabric build-up. Sew the binding on with a consistent ¼" seam.

Mitering the corners is easy once you have done it a few times. Follow these steps and your binding will go on smoothly and lay flat.

1. Sew the seam to exactly ¼" from the bottom edge of the quilt. Lift the presser foot and pull the quilt away from the sewing machine.
2. Fold the binding up and away from the quilt at a 45° angle *(Figure 6)*.
3. Now fold the binding back down *(Figure 7)*.
4. Carefully place the needle ¼" in from both sides of the corner, line up the binding with the outer edge of the quilt and continue sewing along the next side.
5. Continue around the entire quilt in this manner, stopping about 4" away from your first stitches. Remove the quilt completely from the sewing machine and lay it on a flat surface.
6. Now, join the two ends. Lay both ends along the edge of the quilt, overlapping them *(Figure 8)*.

Draw a pencil line along the edge of the binding that is on top. Add ½" beyond the pencil line and cut off the extra binding. Line up the two ends and hold them in position with a pin. Now join the ends with a ¼" seam allowance and finger-press the seams open *(Figure 9)*. Finish stitching the binding in place.

Once the binding is sewn on completely, lay the quilt right side up on your cutting mat. Lay a quilter's ruler along the edge of the quilt and, with your rotary cutter, trim the backing and batting to exactly ¼" beyond the seam. Take your time and do this accurately so that the binding will be filled with a consistent amount of backing and batting. Fold the binding over the back of the quilt, roll the seam allowance under and blindstitch it in place.

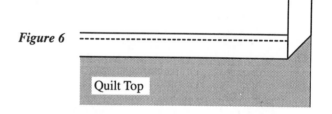

Figure 6

Quilt Top

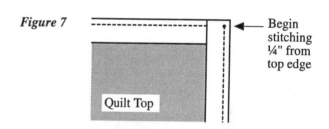

Figure 7

← Begin stitching ¼" from top edge

Quilt Top

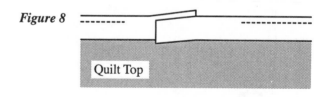

Figure 8

Quilt Top

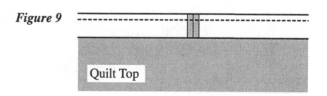

Figure 9

Quilt Top

Sign and Date Your Quilt:

Don't forget to sign and date your quilt when you are done. You can embroider your name and date, or make a separate label and attach it to the back of your quilt.

Linden Mill

17" x 19"
4" blocks - 4 blocks set on point

Shown on inside back cover

Templates needed:

B, J, N, O

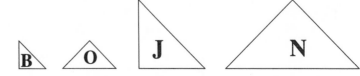

Linden Mill

This top was made by Mary Schafer. This is a special quilt in my collection because Mary used this pattern in the very first pieced quilt she made. Mary is an important figure in the quilt world and has been my good friend for many years. The dark triangles in the four blocks were cut from two red prints. One of these prints, a large floral, was used for the outer border.

Cutting Instructions:
Choose either templates or rotary cutting.

Template	Per Block	Total
B	8 light, 8 dark	32 light, 32 dark
O	4 light, 4 dark	16 light, 16 dark
J		4 light
N		4 light

Rotary

Small triangles -
    cut 16 1-7/8" squares from both light and dark fabric, cut diagonally
Large triangles -
    cut 4 3¼" squares from both light and dark fabric, cut diagonally twice
Corner triangles -
    cut 2 3¾" squares, cut diagonally
Fill-in triangles -
    cut 1 7-1/8" square, cut diagonally twice

For either method, cut one 4½" square for center block

Borders

Inner: Top & bottom (cut two) - 1¾" x 12",
        Sides (cut two) - 1¾" x 14½"
Outer: Sides (cut two) - 2" x 14½",
        Top & bottom (cut two) - 3" x 17½"

To Assemble:

Refer to General Instructions for tips for sewing triangles. Make four blocks by sewing two light and two dark small triangles (**B**) together. Sew one light and one dark large triangle (**O**). Connect these two units (*Figure 1*). Repeat to make four units. Sew together to make one block (*Figure 2*). Repeat to make four blocks. Sew blocks, fill-in triangles (**N**), center square and corner triangles (**J**) in rows as shown in *Figure 3*. Add top and bottom inner borders, inner side borders. Add outer side borders and top & bottom outer borders. Finish quilt following General Directions.

Figure 1

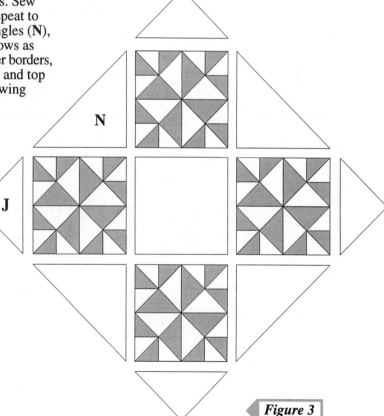

Figure 3

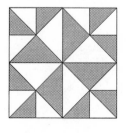

Figure 2

Sawtooth

16" x 20"
4" block - 12 blocks set 3 x 4

Shown on inside front cover

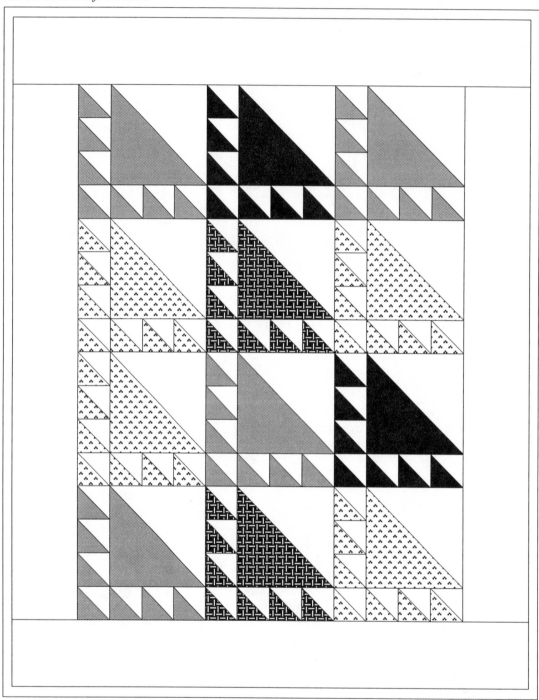

Templates needed:

B, K

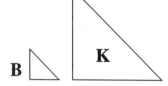

Sawtooth

Here is one of the great traditional patterns made with triangles. I made it with reproduction prints for an old-fashioned look.

Cutting Instructions:

Choose either templates or rotary cutting.

Template	Per Block	Total
B	7 light, 7 dark	84 light, 84 dark
K	1 light, 1 dark	12 light, 12 dark

Rotary

Small triangles -
    cut 42 1-7/8" squares from both light and dark fabric, cut diagonally
Large triangles -
    cut 6 3-7/8" squares from both light and dark fabric, cut diagonally

Borders

Cut four rectangles 2½" x 16½"

To Assemble:

Refer to General Instructions for tips for sewing triangles. Sew a small light triangle (**B**) to a small dark triangle. Press seam to the dark and trim off points. Repeat to make a total of seven triangle-squares. Sew three together to make a unit. Sew four together to make another unit. Sew a large light triangle (**K**) to a large dark triangle. Press seam allowance to the dark and trim off points. Add the three-triangle-square unit to one side of the large unit. Add the four-triangle-square unit to the bottom of the unit (*Figure 1*). Repeat to make 12 blocks.

Lay out the blocks in four rows of three blocks each (*Figure 2*). Sew the blocks into rows, then sew the rows together. Add the borders to the sides then to the top and bottom. Finish the quilt following the General Instructions.

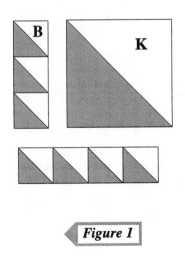

Figure 1

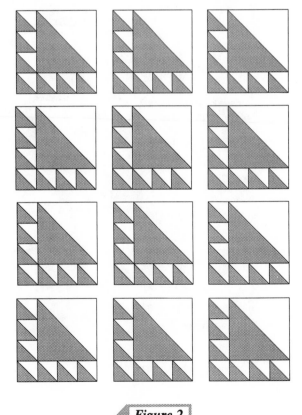

Figure 2

Patch as Patch Can

15" x 18"
3" blocks - 30 blocks set 5 x 6

Shown on inside back cover

Templates needed:

B, G

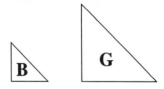

Patch as Patch Can

Another name for this pattern is Corn and Beans. I've always liked blue and white quilts. This color scheme was particularly popular around 1840. I made my quilt with a blue pin-dot and unbleached muslin. This was tricky to make and I assume that is why it is was so named. The most important thing to remember when making this quilt is to pay attention. If you don't, it is easy to turn the triangles the wrong direction and then you have to get out your ripper. Pressing is important, and working in an organized way is very helpful.

Cutting Instructions:
Choose either templates or rotary cutting.

Template	Per Block	Total
B	5 light, 5 dark	150 light, 150 dark
G	1 light, 1 dark	30 light, 30 dark

Rotary

Small triangles -
    cut 75 1-7/8" squares from both light
    and dark fabric, cut diagonally
Large triangles -
    cut 15 2-7/8" squares from both
    light and dark fabric, cut diagonally

To Assemble:

Refer to General Instructions for tips for sewing triangles. This block will be constructed in a different manner than most. Sew three dark and two light small triangles (**B**) together (*Figure 1*). Sew three light and two dark small triangles together as also shown in *Figure 1*. Join these two units, matching the triangles. Add a large light and dark triangle (**G**) (*Figure 2*) to the small triangle unit (*Figure 3*). Repeat to make four blocks. Join these four together as shown in *Figure 4*. Make a total of six four-block units. You will also need three two-block units. Sew two four-block units and one two-block unit together to make a row.

Repeat to make three rows total (*Figure 5*). Sew the rows together. Finish quilt following the General Instructions.

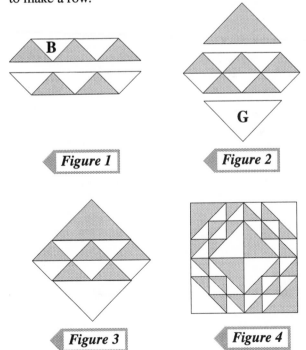

Figure 1

Figure 2

Figure 3

Figure 4

Figure 5

Baby Triangles

15" x 18"

Shown on inside back cover

Templates needed:

R, CC

Baby Triangles

Here each triangle is split in half, with the top half being a print. The tiny triangles seem to float on the white background.

Cutting Instructions:

The pieced triangles will be cut from pieced fabric. Use the template to cut out both the pieced triangle and the plain triangle.

Template	Total
R	40 pieced, 40 plain
CC	4 pieced, 4 plain
CC (reversed)	4 pieced, 4 plain (See assembly directions for how to make pieced fabric.)

Borders

Side: Cut two rectangles 2½" x 14½"
Top & Bottom: Cut two rectangles 2½" x 15½"

To Cut Triangles R, CC & CC (reversed):

Triangles **R, CC & CC(r)** will be cut from pieced fabric. To create the "fabric", you will need 1½" strips from color scraps and a background fabric. Cut across the width of the fabric (usually 40").

Background: Cut four 1½" strips, 40" long
Color: Cut 1½" strips, various lengths
           Total amount will be about 150"

Sew together background and color strips. Press seam to dark fabric. Place template **R** on top of fabric, matching guide line to seam line. Cut out triangles (*Figure 1*). Repeat for **CC** and **CC(r)**

To Assemble:

Refer to General Instructions for tips for sewing triangles. There will be a total of eight rows, each row having five plain and five pieced triangles **R**. The rows will begin and end with **CC** and **CC (r)**. (*Figure 2*). After the rows are pieced, lay two rows out so the bottom point of the first plain triangle meets the top point of the first pieced triangle. Sew four sets of these rows, then sew the two-row units together (*Figure 2*). Add the side borders, then the top and bottom borders. Finish the quilt following the General Directions.

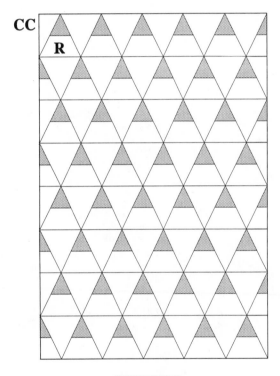

CC

R

Figure 2

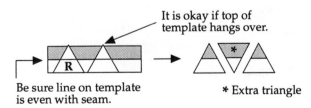

It is okay if top of template hangs over.

Be sure line on template is even with seam.

* Extra triangle

Figure 1

*You will end up with a set of triangles with the opposite color arrangement. Save these! They could be used to make other designs.

The Spy

14" x 18"
2" blocks - 63 blocks set 7 x 9

Shown on inside back cover

Template needed:

G

The Spy

Most of the triangle-squares are made of brown and black, with just a few other tones added for interest. The units are then sewn together randomly, creating a variety of new shapes. A variety of tans and golds were used for the light side of the square. Blacks, dark navy and one red was used for the dark side.

Template	Per Block	Total
G	1 light, 1 dark	63 light, 63 dark

Rotary

Cut 32 light and 32 dark 2-7/8" squares, cut diagonally

Cutting Instructions:

Choose either templates or rotary cutting.

To Assemble:

Refer to General Instructions for tips for sewing triangles. Sew a light triangle (**G**) to a dark triangle (**G**). Press seam to the dark and trim off points (*Figure 1*). Repeat to make a total of 63 triangle-square blocks. Lay out the blocks to make a pleasing arrangement of nine rows of seven blocks. Sew blocks together to make rows and sew rows together (*Figure 2*). A fun way to do this is to shuffle the blocks and just randomly pick one up to add to the row. It will be a total surprise! Finish the quilt following the General Instructions.

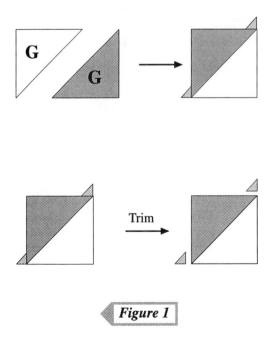

Figure 1

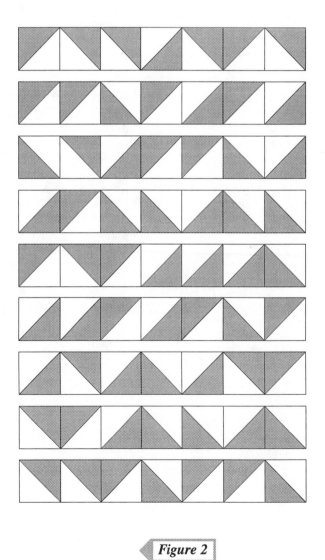

Figure 2

Birds in Flight

18¼" x 20-1/8"
3-3/8" blocks - 20 blocks set 4 x 5

Shown on inside back cover

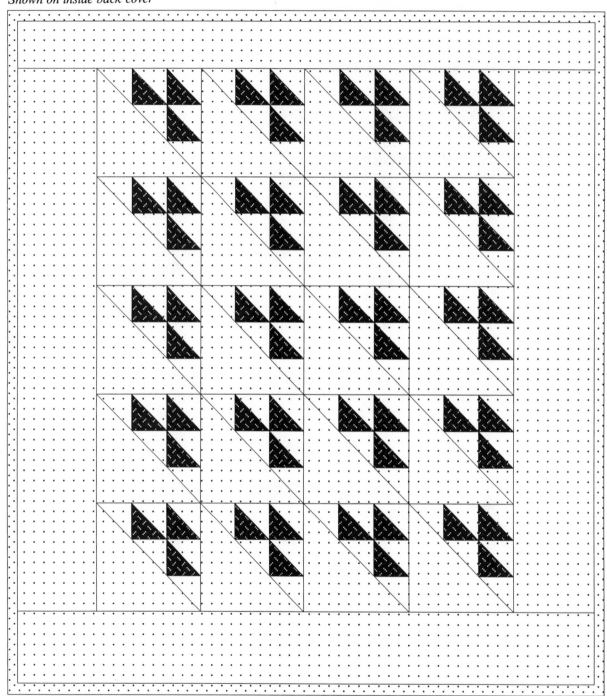

Templates needed:

C, Z

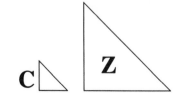

Birds in Flight

Here is an orderly little quilt. I used a blue print for the birds and a soft tan print with trees on it. The birds are in flight and flying high above the trees.

Cutting Instructions:

Choose either templates or rotary cutting. Cut all the small dark triangles from one fabric. The rest of the pieces were cut from the same light fabric.

Template	Per Block	Total
C	6 light, 3 dark	120 light, 60 dark
Z	1 light	20 light

Rotary

Small triangles -
   dark: cut 30 2" squares, cut diagonally
   light: cut 60 2" squares, cut diagonally
Large triangles -
   cut 10 4¼" squares, cut diagonally

Borders

Top: Cut one rectangle 1¾" x 18¾"
Sides: Cut two rectangles 2-7/8" x 17-3/8"
Bottom: Cut one rectangle 2½" x 18¾"

To Assemble:

Refer to General Instructions for tips for sewing triangles. Sew a small light triangle (**C**) to a small dark triangle. Press seam to the dark and trim off points. Repeat to make a total of three triangle-squares. Sew together with three light triangles to form a unit (*Figure 1*). Sew this unit to one large triangle (**Z**) to make a block. Repeat to make twenty blocks. Lay out blocks in five rows of four blocks each (*Figure 2*). Sew the blocks together to make rows, then sew the rows together. Add the side borders, then add the top and bottom borders. Finish quilt following the General Instructions.

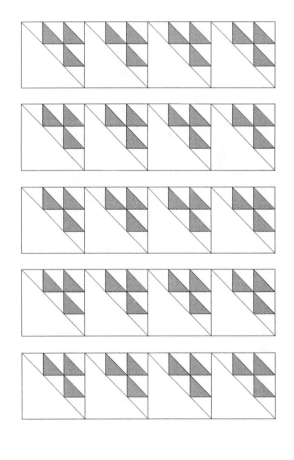

Figure 2

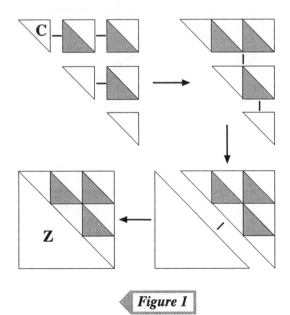

Figure 1

Flock of Geese

18" x 20"
4" block - 12 blocks set 3 x 4

Shown on inside back cover

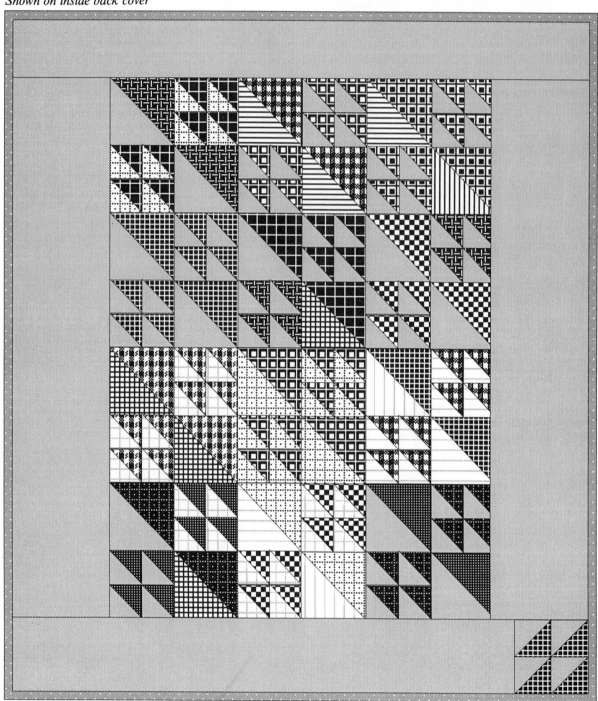

Templates needed:

B, C, G

20

Flock of Geese

I chose plaids for an outdoors look that seemed in keeping with the name of this pattern. It always thrills me to see and hear a flock of migrating geese flying over my house.

Cutting Instructions:

The borders and some of the small and large triangles were cut from the same plaid fabric. The rest of the triangles were cut from a variety of light and dark plaids. Choose either templates or rotary cutting.

Template	Per Block	Total
B	8 light, 8 dark	96 light, 96 dark
G	2 light, 2 dark	24 light, 24 dark
C		4 light, 4 dark

Rotary

Small triangles - Cut 48 1-7/8" squares of both light and dark, cut diagonally
Large triangles - Cut 12 2-7/8" squares of both light and dark, cut diagonally
Border triangles - Cut 2 2" squares of of both light and dark, cut diagonally

Borders

Top: Cut one rectangle 2¼' x 18½"
Sides: Cut two rectangles 3½" x 16½"
Bottom: Cut one rectangle 2¾" x 16¼"

To Assemble:

Refer to General Instructions for tips for sewing triangles. Sew a small light triangle (**B**) to a small dark triangle. Press seam towards the dark. Trim off points. Repeat to make eight triangle-square units. Sew four together to make one unit (*Figure 1*). Make two of these units. Sew a large light triangle (**G**) to a large dark triangle (**G**). Press seam towards the dark. Trim off points. Repeat to make two units. Sew these together with the other two units to make a block (*Figure 2*). Repeat these steps to make a total of 12 blocks. Lay out the blocks in four rows of three blocks (*Figure 3*). Sew blocks together to make rows then sew the rows together. Make one more unit of the medium sized triangles by sewing a light triangle (**C**) to a dark triangle. Press and trim points. Repeat to make four triangle-square units. Sew together. Add to the right side of the bottom border. Sew side borders on, then add the top and bottom borders. Finish the quilt following the General Instructions.

Figure 1

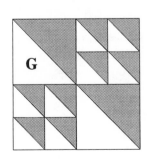

Figure 2

Figure 3

Kansas Troubles

18" x 20"
4" blocks - 16 blocks set 4 x 4

Shown on inside back cover

Templates needed:

B, G, L

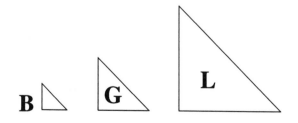

Kansas Troubles

I made this quilt as sweet as I could because I have sweet memories of growing up in Kansas. I have always wanted to make this pattern because I like the name of it and I think it is a beautiful block. Remembering very well the soft colors of Kansas, I made this quilt with a variety of my favorite bubble gum pinks and tans.

Cutting Instructions:

Choose either templates or rotary cutting.

Template	Per Block	Total
B	6 light, 6 dark	96 light, 96 dark
G	1 medium	16 medium
L	1 light	16 light

Rotary

Small triangles -
   Cut 48 light and 48 dark 1-7/8" squares,
      cut diagonally
Medium triangles -
   Cut 8 2-7/8" squares, cut diagonally
Large triangles -
   Cut 8 4-7/8" squares, cut diagonally

Borders

Sides: Cut two rectangles 1½" x 16½"
Top & Bottom: Cut two rectangles 2½" x 18½"

To Assemble:

Refer to General Instructions for tips for sewing triangles. Sew a small light triangle (**B**) to a small dark triangle. Press seam to the dark and trim off points. Repeat to make a total of four triangle-squares. Sew two units together. Add a dark triangle to one end (*Figure 1*) . Sew two small light triangles together. Join this to the remaining two light-dark triangle-squares and add a dark triangle to one end (*Figure 2*). Sew these two units to the medium triangle (**G**). Add the large triangle (**L**) to finish up the block (*Figure 3*). Repeat to make 16 blocks. Sew four blocks together as shown in *Figure 4*. Make four of these large units and sew them together. Add the side borders. Sew the top and bottom borders on to finish the top. Complete the quilt following the General Instructions.

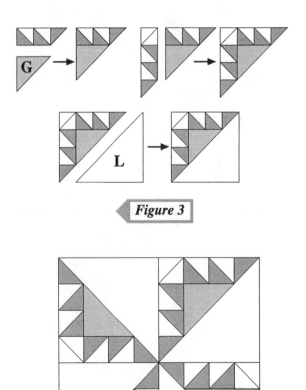

Figure 3

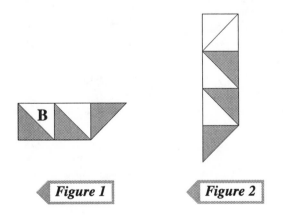

Figure 1

Figure 2

Figure 4

Charm Quilt 18" x 21-7/8"

Shown on inside front cover

Templates needed:

S, U

 S   **U**   **U** (reversed)

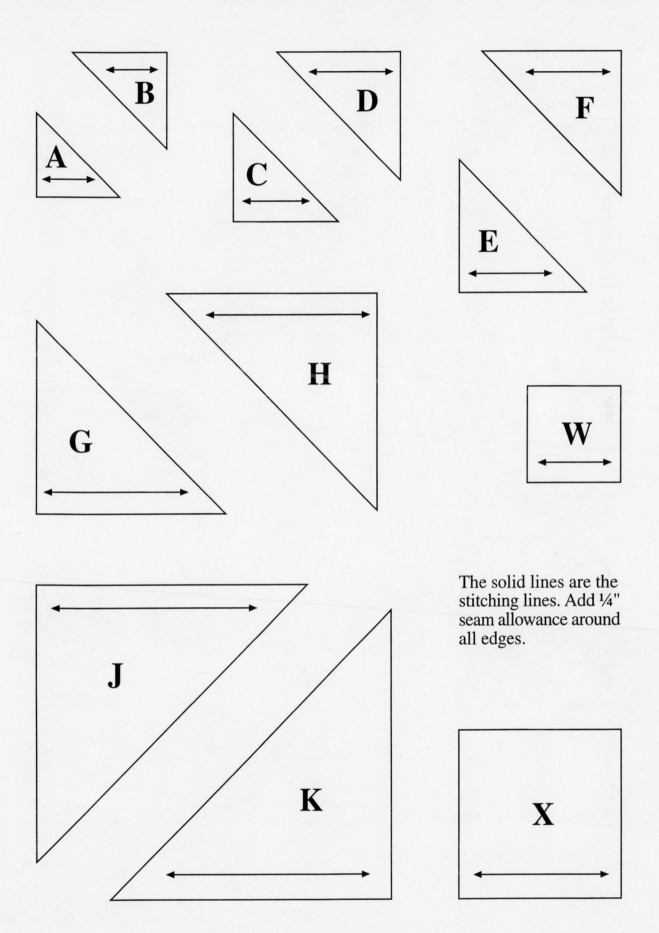

The solid lines are the stitching lines. Add ¼" seam allowance around all edges.

Plate 1

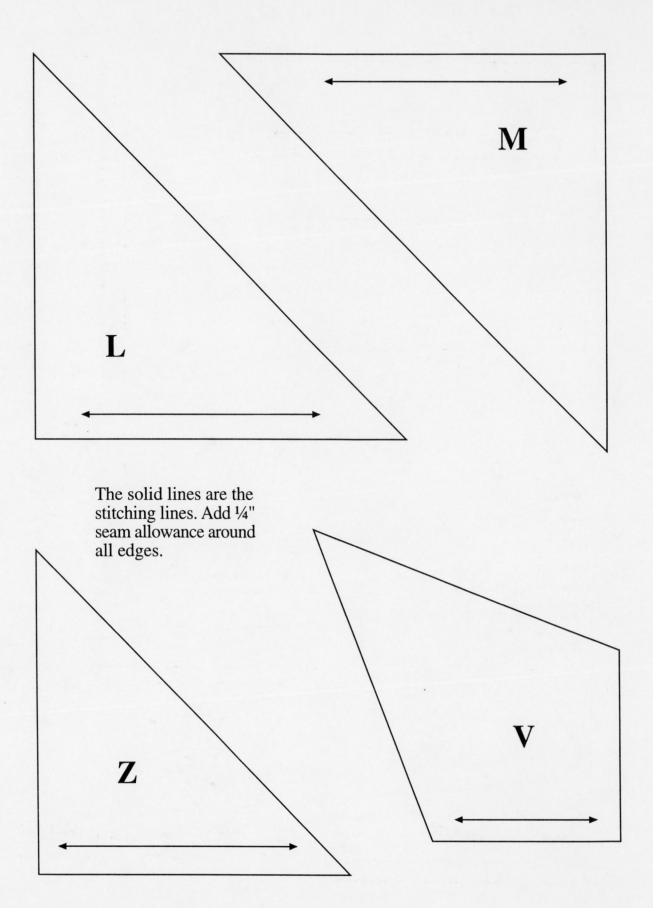

M

L

The solid lines are the
stitching lines. Add ¼"
seam allowance around
all edges.

Z

V

Plate   2

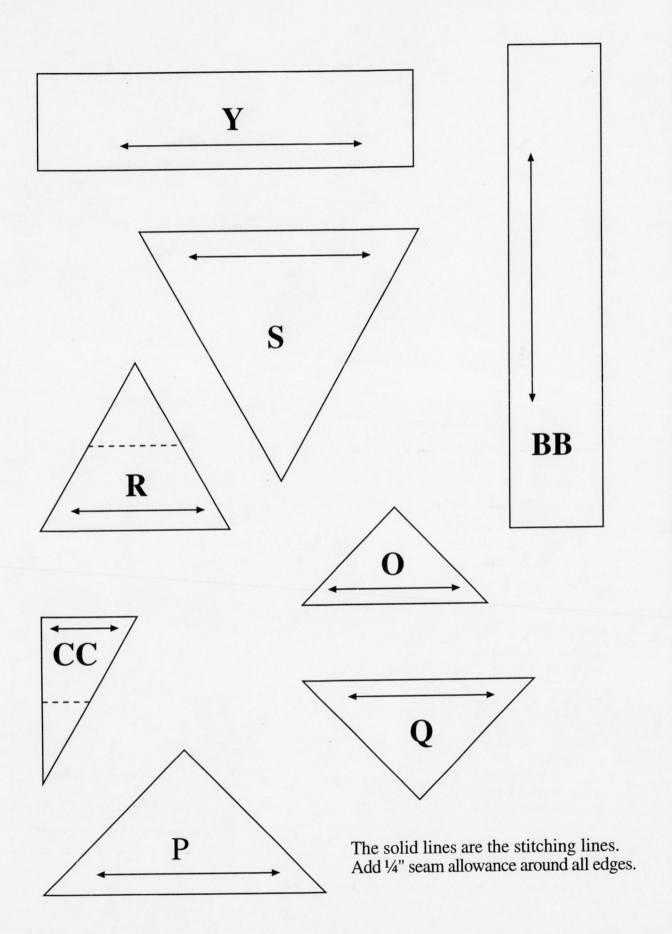

The solid lines are the stitching lines.
Add ¼" seam allowance around all edges.

Plate 3

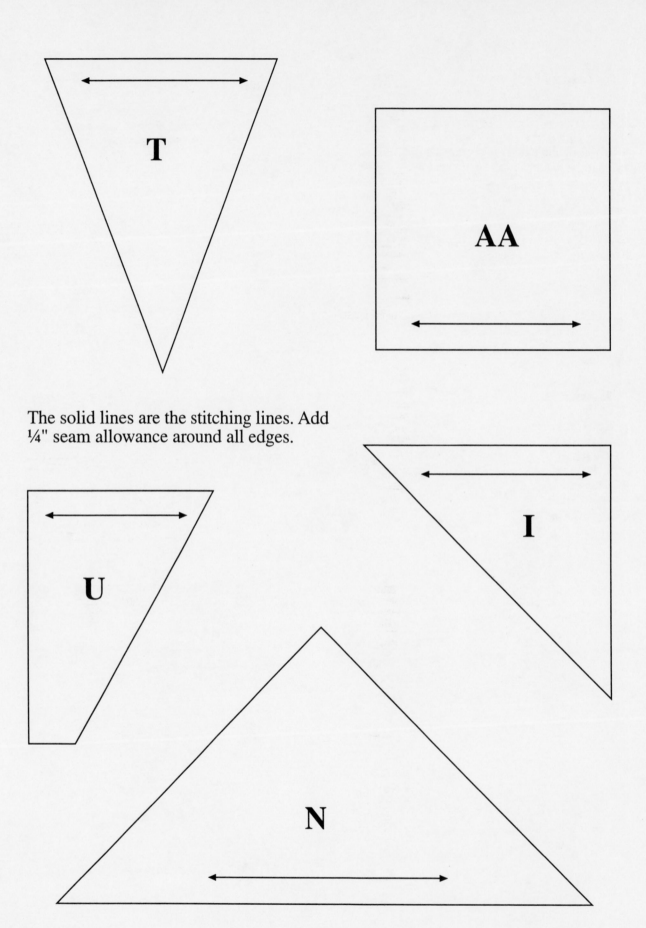

T

AA

The solid lines are the stitching lines. Add ¼" seam allowance around all edges.

U

I

N

Plate 4

Charm Quilt

To qualify as a charm quilt, every single patch must be a different fabric. This pattern, Thousand Triangles (also called Thousand Pyramids), was one of the most popular patterns for charm quilts. For this quilt, I cut the patches and then sewed them together randomly. That is, I sewed them together without any regard for color placement. The prints are all wonderful and they work together in any arrangement. The side half-triangles are generous on the small end. They could come to an exact point, but I left a base instead of a point.

Cutting Instructions:
You will need 70 different prints to make this quilt. Only a small amount of each fabric is used (just enough to cut out one triangle!).

Template	Total
S	56 of different fabrics
U	8 of different fabrics
U(reversed)	6 of different fabrics

Borders	
Sides:	Cut two rectangles 2¼" x 18-7/8"
Top and Bottom:	Cut two rectangles 2¼" x 17½"

To Assemble:

Refer to General Instructions for tips for sewing triangles. This quilt is constructed in seven rows. There are eight complete triangles in each row with "half" triangles at the begining and end. Lay out the patches in rows. These triangles (**S**) are easiest to sew together if you line them up, right sides together and join them in two's, then four's and so on. Be careful to start and end each row with the correct "half" triangle (**U**) (regular or reversed). Sew together to make rows. When sewing the rows together, try to match the points where three triangles from one row and three from the other row come together. Add the side borders, then the top and bottom borders. Finish the quilt following the General Instructions.

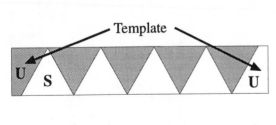
Template

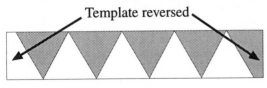
Template reversed

Figure 1

Figure 2

Autumn Triangles

18" x 19½"
1½" blocks - 30 blocks set 5 x 6

Shown on back cover

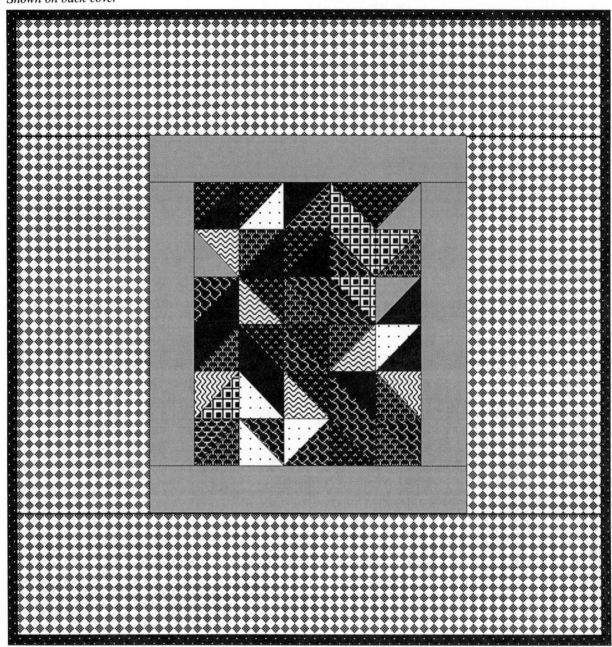

Template needed:

F

Autumn Triangles

Using fall colors, I pieced the triangles together randomly and joined the rows together randomly. The wide outside border is a beautiful leaf print.

Template	Total
F	60

Rotary

Cut 30 2-3/8" squares, cut diagonally

Borders

Inner: Sides: Cut two 2" x 9½" rectangles
Top & bottom: Cut two 2" x 11" rectangles
Outer: Sides: Cut two 4¼" x 12½" rectangles
Top & bottom: Cut two 4¼" x 18½" rectangles

Cutting Instructions:

Choose either templates or rotary cutting.

To Assemble:

Refer to General Instructions for tips for sewing triangles. Sew two triangles together (**F**). Press seam to the dark and trim off points (*Figure 1*). Repeat to make a total of 30 triangle-squares. Sew five units together randomly to make a row. Repeat to make six rows total (*Figure 2*). Sew rows together. Add inner border, sewing sides on first, then adding the top and bottom. Repeat sequence to add outer border. Finish quilt following General Instructions.

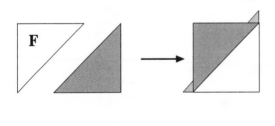

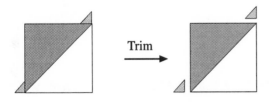

Trim

Figure 1

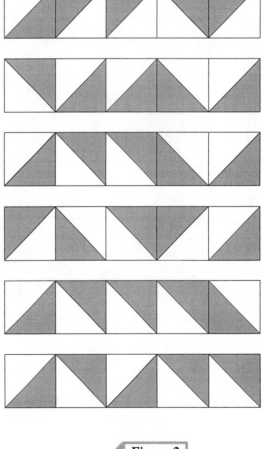

Figure 2

Rocky Glen

16" x 18"
3½" blocks - 16 blocks set 4 x 4

Shown on inside back cover

Templates needed:

A, I

Rocky Glen

This quilt is made of a tan print and a green print. The pattern shows up well because of the strong contrast of the prints. You can turn the blocks in different directions to create very different looking patterns.

Cutting Instructions:

Choose either templates or rotary cutting.

Template	Per Block	Total
A	7 light, 7 dark	112 light, 112 dark
I	1 light, 1 dark	16 light, 16 dark

Rotary

Small triangles -
From both light and dark,
cut 56 1¾" squares, cut diagonally
Large triangles -
From both light and dark,
cut 8 3½" squares, cut diagonally

Borders

Sides: Cut two rectangles 1½" x 14½"
Top & Bottom: Cut two rectangles 2½" x16½"

To Assemble:

Refer to General Instructions for tips for sewing triangles. Sew a small light triangle (**A**) to a small dark triangle (**A**). Press seam to the dark and trim off points. Repeat to make a total of seven triangle-squares. Sew three together to make a unit. Sew four together to make another unit, being careful to notice the orientation of the dark triangle (*Figure 1*). Sew a large light triangle (**I**) to a large dark triangle (**I**). Press seam allowance to the dark and trim off points. Add the three-triangle-square unit to one side of the large unit. Add the four-triangle-square unit to the top of the unit (*Figure 2*). Repeat to make 16 blocks.

Put four blocks together to make one large unit (*Figure 3*). Repeat to make four large units. Sew these together. Add side borders, then add the top and bottom. Finish quilt following the General Instructions.

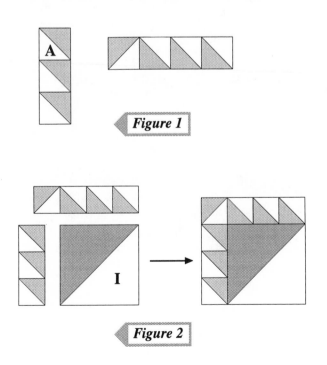

Figure 1

Figure 2

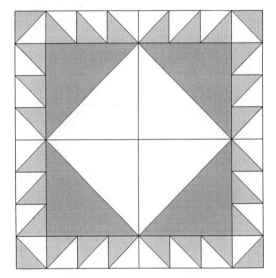

Figure 3

Medallion

15" x 17½"

Shown on inside back cover

Template needed:

Q

Medallion

This quilt is a small version of an antique quilt. The medallion effect is created by arranging the colors in rounds of dark and light.

Cutting Instructions:

Choose either templates or rotary cutting.

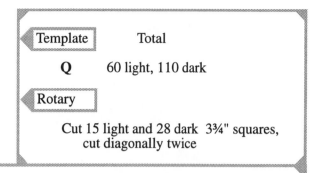

Template	Total
Q	60 light, 110 dark

Rotary	
	Cut 15 light and 28 dark 3¾" squares, cut diagonally twice

To Assemble:

Refer to General Instructions for tips for sewing triangles. Lay out rows so you can get the arrangement you want. Begin in the middle with four triangles pieced together. Add triangles as shown.

Piece the triangles in rows before adding to the center section. Piece two triangles to make a corner triangle. Add units in numerical order as shown below.

Star Puzzle

16" x 20"
4" blocks - 10 pieced, 10 plain, 4 x 5

Shown on inside front cover

Templates needed:

B, L, Q

Star Puzzle

Change the effect of this star block by using one print only or a combination of prints in the block. One way to work is to make a bunch of center pinwheel units, a bunch of star point units and a bunch of corner units and then arrange and rearrange them as you like. In my quilt, the corner triangles are a variety of bubble gum pinks, the blocks are in browns and yellow primarily. One block has red star points, one block has a black pinwheel, and one has a red pinwheel. These little changes add variety to the quilt. Make ten alternate blocks and play with them until you like the arrangement. Four different pinks were used for the corner triangles and one corner triangle is turned the wrong way.

Choose either templates or rotary cutting.

Template	Per Block	Total
B	24 total -	240
	8 light, 4 corner	80, 40
	4 center, 8 star points	40, 80
O	4 light	40
L	1 light, 1 color	10, 10

Rotary

Small triangles -
    cut 120 1-7/8" squares, cut diagonally
Medium triangles -
    cut 10 3-1/4" squares,
        cut diagonally twice
Large triangles -
    cut 10 4-7/8" squares, cut diagonally

To Assemble:

Refer to General Instructions for tips for sewing triangles. Sew a small light triangle (**B**) to a small corner triangle (**B**). Press seam to the dark and trim off points. Repeat to make a total of four triangle-squares. Sew two star-point triangles (**B**) to medium triangle (**O**). Repeat to make four units. Sew a light triangle (**B**) to a center triangle (**B**). Repeat to make four triangle-squares. Sew together to make a pinwheel (*Figure 1*). Add two-star point units to two sides of pinwheel (*Figure 2*). Sew two corner units to a star-point unit. Repeat. Sew these units to center pinwheel unit to complete block (*Figure 3*). Repeat to make a total of ten blocks.

Make alternate blocks by sewing one light large triangle (**L**) to a colored triangle (**L**). Repeat to make ten blocks total. Lay out the pieced and alternate blocks to make a pleasing arrangement. Sew together to make rows, then sew rows together to make the top (*Figure 4*). Finish quilt following the General Instructions.

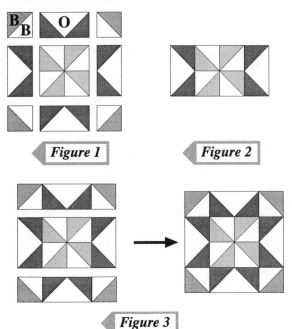

Figure 1

Figure 2

Figure 3

Figure 4

Wild Goose Chase

19" x 21"
42 units set in bars

Shown on inside front cover

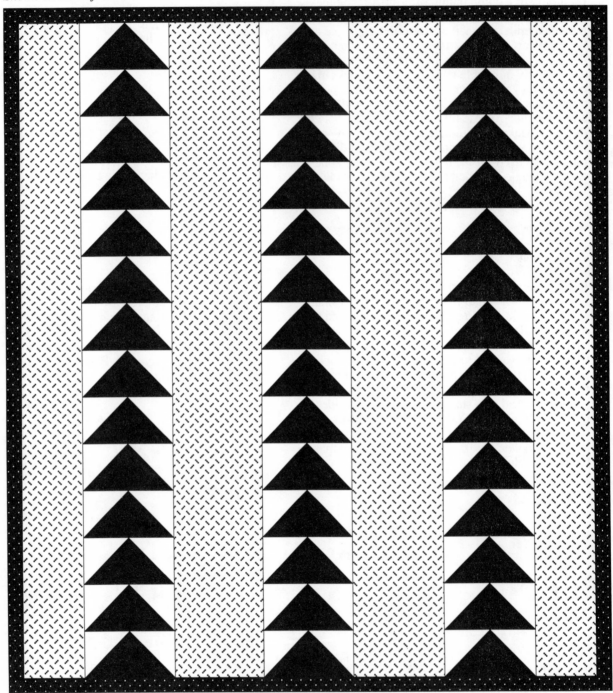

Templates needed:

F, P

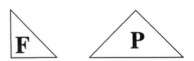

Wild Goose Chase

I think of Wild Goose Chase as one of the great classical quilt designs coming to us from the tradition. I made mine with a wide variety of brown prints and a variety of reproduction shirting prints.

Cutting Instructions:

Small triangles were cut from an assortment of shirting prints. The large triangles were cut from a variety of brown prints. The four long bars were cut from the same larger floral print. Choose either templates or rotary cutting.

Template	Per Unit	Total
F	2 light	84
P	1 dark	42

Rotary

Small triangles -
    cut 42 2-3/8" squares, cut diagonally
Large triangles -
    cut 11 4¼" squares, cut diagonally twice

Bars

Cut two rectangles 3½" x 21½" for inner bars.
Cut two rectangles 2½" x 21½" for outer bars.

To Assemble:

Refer to General Instructions for tips for sewing triangles. Make 42 triangle units for rows. Chain piece the small triangles (**F**) to the large triangle (**P**). Add the small triangle to the right side as shown in *Figure 1*. Finger press the small triangle up (*Figure 2*). Add the small triangle to the left side (*Figure 3*) and finger press the small triangle up. Trim points off (*Figure 4*).

Sew 14 of these units together to make a row. Stitch with the big triangle (wrong side) pointing to the right facing up (*Figure 5*). This will allow you to see where the stitching lines cross. Stitch just to the right of this intersection. Press all seams up. Repeat to make three rows.

Lay out the bar rectangles and pieced rows referring to large drawing. Sew rows together. Finish quilt following General Directions.

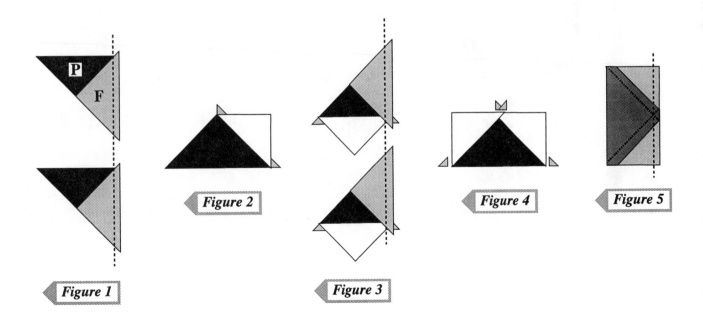

Figure 1   *Figure 2*   *Figure 3*   *Figure 4*   *Figure 5*

String of Triangles

18" x 20"
90 units set 9 x 10

Shown on inside front cover

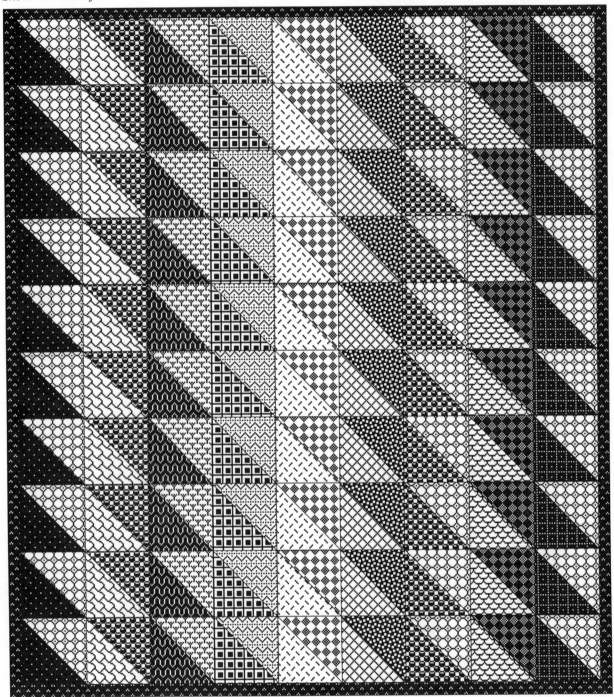

Template needed:

G

String of Triangles

This scrap quilt is made with half-square triangles arranged so the colors run vertically. One side of the triangle unit is consistently the same print in each row. The other side of all triangle units is consistently tan, though ten different tan prints were used. Using different tan prints contributes to the scrappy appearance. Every other row is flip-flopped.

Cutting Instructions:

Cut half the triangles from one color. A variety of tan prints were used. To make the "string", cut enough triangles of one color for each row. Choose either templates or rotary cutting.

Template	Per Unit	Total
G	1 tan, 1 color	90 tan, 90 colors

(for each vertical row, cut ten of one color. There are nine rows.)

Rotary

Tan triangles (90 total):
   Cut 45 2 7/8" squares, cut diagonally.

Colored triangles (90 total):
   Cut five 2 7/8" squares, cut diagonally.
   Repeat for a total of nine sets of ten triangles, using different colors for each set.

To Assemble:

Refer to General Instructions for tips for sewing triangles. Sew tan and colored triangles (**G**)and press towards the color (*Figure 1*). Try to stay consistent in your pressing. Join ten units into a row and press all seams up. Repeat to make a total of nine rows. Every other row is flipped upside down to create the pattern (*Figure 2*). Lay the rows out and sew rows together. Finish quilt following the General Instructions.

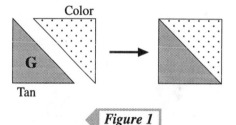

Figure 1

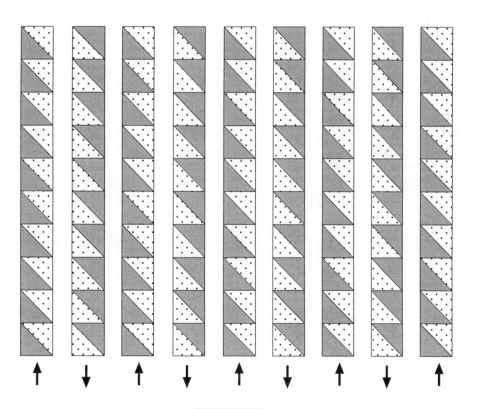

Figure 2

The Pinks Are Up   15" x 19½"

Shown on inside front cover

Templates needed:

F, P

The Pinks Are Up

The green print is consistent throughout this quilt while the pinks are a variety of prints. They are not arranged in particular order, but allowed to bounce around the surface of the quilt freely.

Cutting Instructions:

Choose either templates or rotary cutting.

Template	Per Row	Total
F	2 yellow	24
P	4 pink, 5 green	48 pink, 60 green

Rotary

Small triangles -
      cut 12 2-3/8" squares, cut diagonally
Large triangles -
      cut 12 pink, 15 green 4¼" squares,
          cut diagonally twice

Borders

Cut two rectangles 1¼" x 15½"

To Assemble:

Refer to General Instructions for tips for sewing triangles. This quilt top is made in rows. Refer to *Figure 1* for how to make a row. Sew a pink triangle (**P**) to a green triangle (**P**). Press seam to the dark and trim off points. Repeat to make a total of 48 triangle units. Sew two units together to make a unit of four triangles. Repeat to make 24 units of four. Sew two of these together. Add one green triangle on the end. Add two yellow triangles (**F**) to make one row. Repeat to make 12 rows. Sew the rows together (*Figure 2*). Add the top and bottom borders. Finish the quilt following the General Instructions.

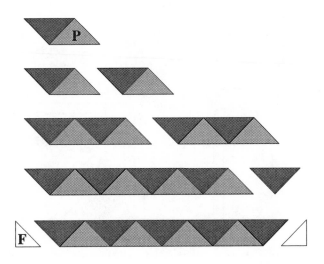

Figure 1	Figure 2

Triangle Block with Triangle Border

19" x 21½"
2½" blocks - 30 blocks, set 5 x 6

Shown on inside front cover

Templates needed:

AA, Q, T, V

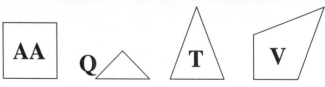

Triangle Block with Triangle Border

Here is a simple triangle block set with alternate plain blocks of old Laura Ashley prints I've had for years. The idea for this quilt came from a quilt made around 1850.

Cutting Instructions:

Choose either templates or rotary cutting.

Template	Per Block	Total
AA		15 med.
Q	2 dark, 2 med.	30 dark, 30 med.
T		26 dark, 22 light
V		4 light

Rotary

Small triangles -
    cut 8 3¾" squares, cut diagonally twice
Squares -
    cut 15 3" squares

The border triangles and corner shapes must be cut using the templates.

To Assemble:

Refer to General Instructions for tips for sewing triangles. Sew a small medium triangle (**Q**) to a small dark triangle (**Q**). Press seam to the dark and trim off points. Repeat to make a total of 30 triangle units. Sew two together to make a block (*Figure 1*). Repeat to make 15 blocks. Lay out pieced and plain blocks (**AA**) to make six rows. Sew rows together.

Border: For side borders, sew six large light triangles (**T**) and seven dark triangles (**T**) together. Repeat. For top and bottom, sew five large light triangles (**T**) and six large dark triangles (**T**) together. Add shape (**V**) to both ends. Repeat. Add side borders, stopping ¼" from the end. *Figure 2* shows a detail of that area. Add top and bottom borders, setting in side seams (*Figure 3*). Finish quilt following the General Instructions.

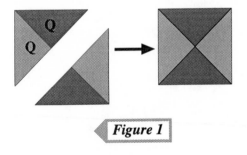

Figure 1

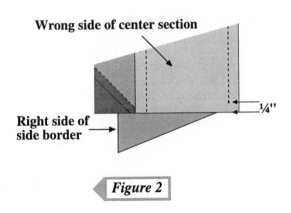

Figure 2

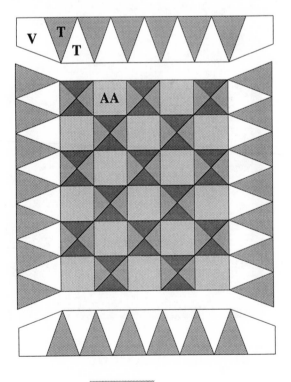

Figure 3

Birds in Air

14" x 19"
4" block - 12 blocks, set 3 x 4

Shown on inside front cover

Templates needed:

D, W, Y

 D   W   Y

Birds in Air

Here is a lively scrap quilt made with a variety of prints and shirtings and set together with sashing and corner squares. A typical Pennsylvania German palette gives this quilt an antique appearance.

Template	Per Block	Total
D	9 light, 9 dark	108 light, 108 dark
W		6
Y		17

Rotary

Cut 2 ¼" strips, recut into 2¼" squares, recut diagonally.
You will need 54 light squares and 54 dark squares

Sashing:

Cut 17 sashing rectangles, 1½" x 4½"
Cut six 1½" x 1½" corner squares

Cutting Instructions:

Dark triangles were cut from a variety of scraps. The light triangles were cut from several shirting prints. The same pink fabric was used for the sashing rectangles and a dark color was used for the corner squares.

To Assemble:

Refer to General Instructions for tips on sewing triangles. Chain piece light triangles (**D**) to dark triangles. Press toward the dark triangle and trim off points (*Figure 1*). Make 108 triangle-square units. Join three units into a row, repeat to make three rows. Join these rows to make a block (*Figure 2*). When you join the rows, make the seams go in opposite directions so there is less bulk. Make sure as you sew that all the triangles are facing the same direction as it is easy to get mixed up. Repeat to make 12 blocks.

Sew the corner squares (**W**) to six of the sashing strips(**Y**) (*Figure 3*). Add sashing to one side of all but one of the blocks as shown in *Figure 4*, noting that the sashing is sewn to one side on eight of the blocks and on a different side on three. One block will not have any sashing. Add the sashing-corner block unit to six of the blocks.

Lay out the blocks in four rows (*Figure 5*). Sew blocks to make rows. Sew rows together. Finish quilt following General Directions.

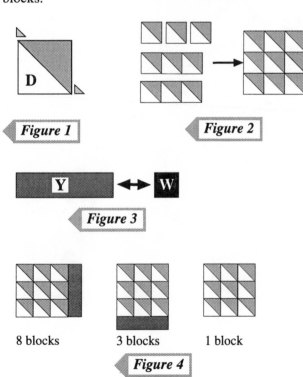

Figure 1

Figure 2

Figure 3

8 blocks   3 blocks   1 block

Figure 4

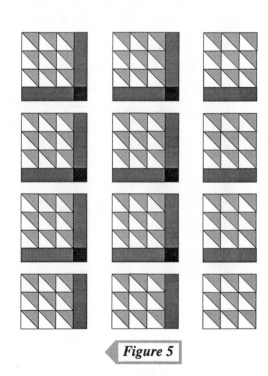

Figure 5

Gwen and Pat's Memorial Triangles

Shown on back cover

15-7/8" x 19¼"
4-1/8" block - 12 blocks set 3 x 4

Templates needed:

E, M, X

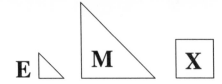

Gwen and Pat's Memorial Triangles

This quilt was made on March 4, 1996. Pat Holly and I had a day together at her house and we both made versions of this quilt. This quilt is a reminder of a delightful day spent sewing with a friend. This is the only quilt in the book that is machine quilted. I quilted it with bright yellow thread, treating the machine-quilted lines as a subtle embellishment.

Cutting Instructions:

Choose either templates or rotary cutting. A variety of orange and purple prints were used.

Template	Per Block	Total
E	5 light, 4 med.	60 light, 48 med.
M	1 dark	12 dark
X		2 dark

Rotary

Small triangles -
   cut 30 light and 24 medium 2¼" squares,
     cut diagonally
Large triangles -
   cut 6 5" squares, cut diagonally

Borders

Sides: cut two rectangles, 2¼" x 17"
Top: cut one rectangle, 1½" x 16-3/8"
Bottom: cut one rectangle, 2¼" x 12-7/8"

To Assemble:

Refer to General Instructions for tips for sewing triangles. Sew a small light triangle (**E**) to a small medium triangle (**E**). Press seam to the dark and trim off points. Repeat to make a total of three triangle-squares. Lay out the three units with two light triangles (**E**) and one medium triangle (**E**) as shown in *Figure 1*. Sew together a triangle and two units. Sew a triangle and one unit. Sew these two rows together. Add a triangle on the end. Sew this to a large dark triangle (**M**) (*Figure 2*). Repeat to make 12 blocks. Lay out in four rows of three blocks. Sew together to make rows. Sew rows together. Add the side borders. Sew two squares (**X**) to both ends of the bottom border. Add bottom and top borders (*Figure 3*). Finish the quilt following the General Instructions.

Figure 1

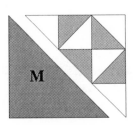

Figure 2

Figure 3

Sampler

18¼" x 21½"
4" blocks - 12 blocks set 3 x 4

Shown on inside front cover

Templates needed:

B, G, Y, BB

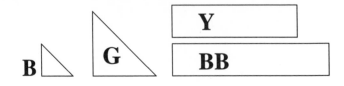

Sampler

Here are twelve different blocks made of triangles. Eleven are traditional blocks and Gwen's Triangles is my original design. At least, I think it is my original design. In the past, I've designed what I thought were original blocks only to discover later that someone else had already thought of it. Any one of these blocks could be used alone to make a triangle quilt.

Cutting Instructions:
Choose either templates or rotary cutting.

Borders

Side borders: cut 2 rectangles 2-5/8" x 19½"
Top & bottom: cut 2 rectangles 1¾" x 18¾"

Template

The blocks use either **B** and/or **G**. Count how many are needed to make your block.

Sashing: **Y**   Cut 8
          BB Cut 9

Rotary

Small triangles:
   cut 1-7/8" squares, cut diagonally
Large triangles:
   cut 2-7/8" squares, cut diagonally
Sashing:
   cut 11 rectangles 1½" x 4½"
   cut 6 rectangles 1½" x 5½"

To Assemble:

Refer to General Instructions for tips for sewing triangles. Use triangles **B** and **G** to make the blocks. Add sashing rectangle **Y** to the side of blocks first, then add larger rectangle **BB** to the bottom. Sew together to make rows. Sew rows together. Add side borders then top and bottom borders. Finish quilt following the General Instructions.

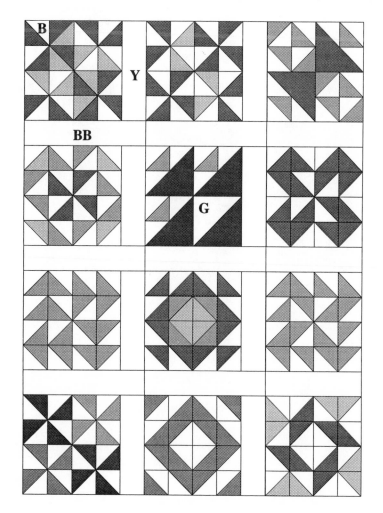

Right to left:

Pinwheel
Simplicity
Double Cross

Gwen's Triangles
Aircraft
Colorado

Return of the Swallows
Magic Triangles
Yankee Puzzle

Scrappy Pinwheel
Diamond Wreath
Balkan Puzzle